FLOWER DRYING

HANDBOOK

*Includes Complete
Microwave Drying
Instructions*

FLOWER DRYING
HANDBOOK

*Includes Complete
Microwave Drying
Instructions*

DOLLY LUTZ MORRIS

*With Microwaving Instructions
by Alice Ensley*

ILLUSTRATIONS
BY CRYSTAL COATES ALLEN

Sterling Publishing Co., Inc. New York
A STERLING/LARK BOOK

Dedicated in loving memory of my mother, Betty Mecca Lutz

Cover Design: Dana Irwin
Editor: Dawn Cusick
Art Direction: Dawn Cusick, Crystal Coates Allen
Production: Elaine Thompson
Proofreading: Julie Brown
Illustrations: Crystal Coates Allen
Location Photography: Gardens of Cynthia Gillooly, Dolly Lutz Morris
  (photographed by Judith Stoll), and Mountain View Nursery.
Arrangement on page 15: Cynthia Gillooly

Library of Congress Cataloging-in-Publication Data
Morris, Dolly Lutz.
    Flower drying handbook : includes complete microwave drying
instructions / Dolly Lutz Morris ; with microwaving instructions by
Alice Ensley.
      p.   cm.
    "A Sterling/Lark book."
    Includes index.
    ISBN 0-8069-4878-7
    1. Flowers--Drying--Handbooks, manuals, etc.   2. Microwave
drying--Handbooks, manuals, etc.   I. Title.
SB 447.M67   1996
635.9'75--dc20   95-37898
                                                    CIP

10 9 8 7 6 5 4 3 2 1

A Sterling/Lark Book

First paperback edition published in 1997 by
Sterling Publishing Company, Inc.
387 Park Avenue South, New York, N.Y. 10016

Produced by Altamont Press, Inc.
50 College Street, Asheville, NC 28801

© 1996 by Altamont Press

Distributed in Canada by Sterling Publishing, % Canadian Manda Group
  One Atlantic Avenue, Suite 105, Toronto, Ontario, Canada M6K 3E7
Distributed in Great Britain and Europe by Cassell PLC
  Wellington House, 125 Strand, London WC2R 0BB, England
Distributed in Australia by Capricorn Link (Australia) Pty Ltd.
  P.O. Box 6651, Baulkham Hills, Business Centre, NSW 2153, Australia

Every effort has been made to ensure that all the information in this
book is accurate. However, due to differing conditions, tools, and
individual skills, the publisher cannot be responsible for any injuries,
losses, and other damages that may result from the use of the
information in this book.

Printed in Hong Kong

Sterling ISBN 0-8069-4878-7 Trade
            0-8069-4879-5 Paper

Contents

Introduction

One of my earliest memories is of sitting on the garden path in the warm sunshine watching my mother tend to her irises. In the spring and summer we would walk through the gardens every morning to see the new blossoms and to select the choicest blooms for harvesting. It seemed a natural part of life. And so the love of flowers has been with me always. Growing flowers is good for the heart and for the soul. Now, many years later, as I walk through the gardens every warm day with my own children, I realize the gift my mother gave to me.

Drying flowers is a wonderful way to extend the pleasures of gardening beyond the warm spring and summer months into a year-round pleasure. The garden begins in early spring when the soil is prepared and planted; summer brings time spent tending the gardens, enjoying their beauty, and picking the harvest of blooms. Then, on a cold fall or winter day, the garden comes to life again when we open boxes of dried flowers to create a wreath or arrangement. Their beauty brings back the garden's sunshine.

This book can be approached in several ways. If you're a long-time gardener anxious to begin drying your own flowers, spend some time reviewing the basic techniques in chapter one. Experienced flower dryers may wish to go directly to the flower profiles for detailed information on landscaping, harvesting, and drying more than 55 flowers. But regardless of how you approach this book, I wish you many summer mornings in your gardens and many winter afternoons of crafting contentment.

Dally Lutz Morris

Harvesting and Drying
Techniques

Drying flowers is one of the simplest, most pleasurable pastimes you will ever undertake. The process is the same with every technique: in one way or another, you simply encourage the moisture found in living flowers to leave. Most drying methods rely on natural evaporation to do the trick, while others techniques, such as microwaving and desiccant drying, evoke the help of science.

To begin, peruse the drying profile of your particular flower. Then ask yourself what type of results you expect, how quickly you expect them, and how much labor you're willing to put into the process. If you're drying the flowers from your best friend's wedding bouquet and want perfect results, then a lightweight desiccant is probably the best choice. If you have space in a nonhumid area just outside your garden, you may well prefer to hang your fresh-cut blooms upside down to dry on your way in from the garden.

Flower harvesting requires good timing and careful selection. Be sure to arrange cut flowers gently in a basket or other container to prevent crushing.

Different varieties of flowers will dry with innumerable variations. Some keep their bright colors, while others darken a shade or two. Some keep their shapes perfectly, while others shrink and curl. These variations are both drastic and subtle, predictable and amazing. Experience will help sharpen your prediction skills, but some flowers will still insist on surprising you.

The first step in drying flowers is the harvesting. Because the ultimate goal in drying flowers is to remove their moisture, it makes sense to avoid picking flowers when they're wet, like after a rain shower or when they're coated in early-morning dew. Blooms with especially dense petals often harbor moisture deep inside; double-check for this moisture before harvesting to prevent the blooms from browning as they dry. Late morning on a sunny day is often the best time, after the sun has had a chance to absorb some of the plant's moisture but before the blooms begin to wilt from intense midday heat. Avoid picking materials with damage from insects or mold, and be sure to harvest more than you anticipate needing to accommodate shrinkage and unsatisfactory results. Refer to the individual profiles for advice on which blooming stage is best for harvesting.

Before drying, you may wish to remove the leaves from the stems. (Some people find most dried leaves very unattractive; an equal number of people adore them.) If you're air-drying, it's just as easy to keep the leaves on and remove

them later if you don't like them. Drying times can vary from as little as three or four days to as long as ten weeks, depending on the method and the original amount of moisture in the flower when it was harvested. Check for dryness frequently to avoid overdrying — a dried flower feels like a flake of breakfast cereal. Store your dried blooms away from sunlight, insects, and moisture. A cardboard box with a tight-fitting lid is ideal.

Air-Drying

Most materials can be dried with one of several air-drying techniques. With these methods, the flower's moisture gently evaporates into the air. There are two nice things about this method. Once you've prepared the blooms, you don't have to do anything else. Just check on their progress every few days to prevent overdrying. The other nice aspect to air-drying is that bunches of drying flowers can become a very appealing part of your home's decor. Choose a drying location that does not receive a lot of sunlight and is not exposed to excess moisture. (The kitchen and bathroom are not good choices.)

Hanging, the oldest of the air-drying techniques, involves securing several stems of the same flower together in a bundle and hanging them upside down to dry. The stems are hung upside down to prevent the weight of petals and leaves from pulling them down into a drooping position. The stems can be secured with clothespins, rubber bands, string, or anything else that will do the job. It makes sense to limit the contents of bundles to flowers of the same type picked in the same blooming stage so their drying times will be the same and you won't have to break bundles apart when only half of the flowers have finished drying. If you have only a few materials, very little space, or know from experience that the materials have similar drying times, you can mix materials.

Another air-drying method, known as screen drying, involves spreading blooms or leaves on a wire screen that has been arranged to provide ventilation on all sides. Prevent excess curling by turning the blooms every day or so. If you want to dry blooms still on their stems, search out a mesh wide enough to accommodate the stem and simply drop the stem through an opening until the bloom rests flat on the screen. This method is a good choice when you're drying single blooms for potpourris or to be hot-glued into a craft project, and for heavy blooms that will not dry well hanging upside down.

Yet another air-drying option is upright-drying. If you're working with a flower that you know dries especially well, such as strawflowers or statice, you can arrange the fresh-cut stems in a pretty vase and allow them to dry in place. Other blooms will dry best when placed in a vase of water and allowed to dry as the water evaporates. The flower profiles will indicate if this method works well.

The fresh-cut yarrow, carnations, roses, and lilies in this arrangement will dry perfectly in place. Just remove the remaining blooms when they're no longer attractive and replace with similar dried flowers.

Bundles of drying flowers can be hung from roof rafters, coat hangers, formal drying racks, or any other object you care to adapt. This adaptation of a garden trellis makes a nice showing.

Screen racks can be made with just a sheet of screening or wire mesh. For more attractive screen racks, consider transforming a piece of furniture.

Desiccants

Desiccants are moisture-absorbing substances such as sand, borax, cornmeal, kitty litter, and silica gel. Although several of these desiccants have been used successfully for centuries, they have been replaced, for the most part, by silica gel. Silica gel granules are lighter in weight and tend to not crush delicate blooms. (If you're working with a sturdy bloom, there's no reason not to use the less expensive materials.) To recycle silica gel, bake the crystals on a foil-covered pan at 200°F (91 C) for 20 minutes, or until the blue, moisture-filled crystals return to their original white or pink color. Desiccant-dried blooms can sometimes reabsorb moisture; you should probably avoid displaying them in a moist environment.

To dry flowers in a desiccant, first sprinkle about an inch (2.5 cm) of desiccant on the bottom of a glass or plastic container. (If working with silica gel, be especially careful not to breathe the dust that will rise up when you pour it. Wearing a mask is a good idea.) Avoid wood and cardboard containers since they can allow moisture in. Arrange the blooms on top of the desiccant with enough space in between blooms to prevent overlapping. Place cup- and bell-shaped blooms on their sides; place other blooms face up. Sprinkle enough desiccant over the blooms to cover the petals. For blooms with multiple rows of petals, gently pull the petals apart and sprinkle in some desiccant to ensure even drying. Double-check for blooms that are bent out of shape. Additional layers of blooms and desiccant can be added if you like.

Novice dryers should limit each container to one type of bloom. Once you've dried a few batches of your favorite blooms and know which ones dry the fastest, you can successfully mix several types of flowers in one container by placing the blooms that take the longest time to dry on the bottom and the ones that take the least time to dry on the top.

Gently check your blooms every three days for dryness and remove them as soon as they're done. Overdrying is especially dangerous with desiccants because the blooms can dry to the point of crumbling into powder. Since desiccant-dried blooms tend to be brittle, handle them carefully, and use a small paintbrush to remove any remaining desiccant.

Desiccant drying has been used for centuries to preserve flower and herb blooms. Lightweight silica gel can absorb more moisture with less bloom damage than most traditional desiccants.

Pressing

Pressing has been around for centuries and is still a good drying choice. Begin by removing the foliage and blooms from the stems, then arrange them on a sheet of blotting paper with space between each material. Double-check for creases and folds in the petals and leaves, then cover them with another sheet of blotting paper and place them between the pages of a thick book or in a flower press. They should be completely dry in six to ten weeks.

Although many serious dryers prefer to use professional flower presses, the traditional technique of placing blooms between sheets of porous paper and then between the pages of a thick book still produces beautiful results.

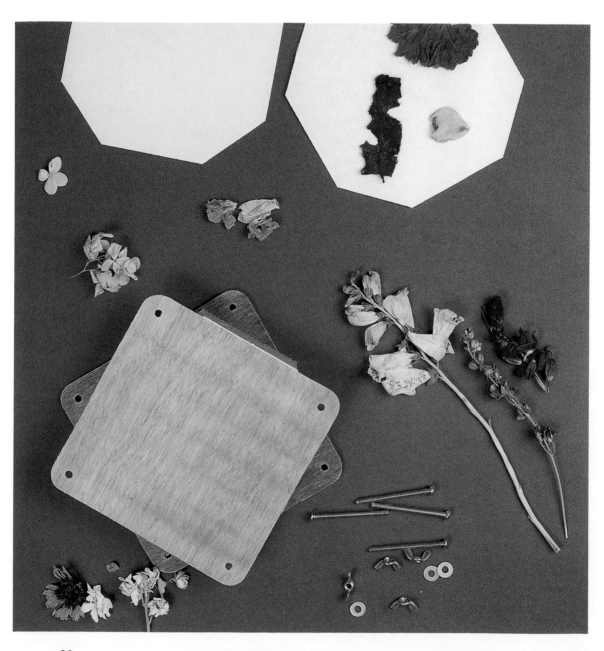

Microwave Drying

Microwave drying is both wondrous and frustrating. Wondrous in that some blooms can be dried with great results in minutes; frustrating in that some drying times and results are predictably unpredictable. Several factors influence the appropriate microwaving times and how good the finished blooms will look.

These factors include the stage of blooming cycle the flower was harvested in, how much moisture was in the bloom, the thickness of individual petals, and the number of blooms being dried at one time. Then there are the complications from variations in microwave wattages and settings. Use the time ranges given in the profiles as guidelines, checking on the blooms halfway through the time range, and then adjust the time up or down depending on your results.

Flowers can be dried between paper towels or in a paper bag. The paper towels absorb the moisture as it leaves the blooms, and they may need to be replaced halfway through the drying process if they're especially wet. Avoid using recycled paper towels since their fibers have a lower combustion temperature. To dry with a paper bag, insert the flowers inside the bag, gently fold up the ends, and place the bag over a microwave-safe bowl. The bowl allows any accumulating moisture to drain downward, instead of dampening the flowers.

Microwave drying makes a time-saving alternative to traditional drying methods. For best results, be prepared to experiment with precise cooking times.

Gardens

Cottage gardens are an easy approach to growing flowers for a beginner. They are meant to seem to have no plan and little organization. Simply choose annuals and perennials that you love. Plant them in drifts of at least three plants of the same type, not in straight rows like soldiers. Try to keep the taller plants toward the back, shorter plants toward the front. It is hard to go wrong in mixing colors since cottage gardens should be bright and cheerful. Arrange the perennials so that various bloom times are spread throughout the bed. Fill in between perennials with annuals for continuous bloom. Cottage gardens give a rather wild, yet charming appearance.

    Rock gardens may be placed anywhere except in dense shade or extremely wet areas; sunny spots are best. Try to give your rock garden a natural appearance, using native rocks as large as can be handled for the best effect. Pads through the rock garden, either flagstone or gravel, add a nice touch. Plants should be mainly perennials, not aggressive spreaders, and a few annuals for season-long color. Place the rocks as they would be in nature, adding pockets of soil for the plants.

    Beds are considered to be a cultivated ares surrounded by an open expanse of lawn and viewed from all sides. Keep the tallest plants toward the middle of the bed and the shortest

toward the outer edges. Beds can be solid annuals, all of one type, or mixed in patterns or rows, or a combination of annuals and perennials.

Mixed borders produce a wonderful display. A border is a planting at the edge of an open area, usually at the property line, in front of a hedge or fence. They are usually viewed only from the front, and may also frame a drive, walk, or open lawn area. Borders should be no more than five feet wide unless they have paths through them so that plants are accessible for tending and harvesting. Included in the mixed border are dutch bulbs, annuals, perennials, roses, and decorative shrubs. The advantages of the mixed border are color and interest over a long period. Plant flowers in drifts of at least three to five of the same type for the best effect. Keep taller plants toward the back of the border. Use annuals to provide season-long color where perennials have ceased their bloom season.

The **cutting garden** is an old-fashioned idea that gives ease of care and harvesting. It could be part of the vegetable garden or an area of its own at the side or back yard. Annuals and perennials in the cutting garden are planted in neat rows, which are easier to mulch, weed, water, and harvest. The cutting of blossoms promotes prolific blooming. Annuals such as strawflowers and tall globe amaranth are best planted in cutting gardens because their leggy appearance isn't particularly attractive in beds and borders. Also include ammobium, nigella, zinnias, and any other flower you like.

Container plantings are a good option for the apartment dweller or person with a small lot. Annuals and perennials grown in containers can provide enough blooms for several wreaths. These could include pots and planters on the patio or balcony, window boxes filled with annuals and perennials, and hanging baskets of mixed annuals.

Cottage gardens like these are good choices for beginners. They do not have to have an elaborate plan or organization. Arrange your plants in drifts of at least three plants of the same type. Avoid straight rows and place taller plants toward the back and shorter plants toward the front.

Glossary

In addition to drying and crafting techniques, the profiles beginning on page 36 include landscaping and growing information. Undoubtedly you will find this information quite helpful, but if you're not an experienced gardener some of the terms may be unfamiliar. The brief list of some commonly used landscaping terms that follows should be helpful for gardening newcomers.

Annual. A plant whose growth cycle is completed in one year. Annuals tend to bloom from shortly after their purchase until the first frost.

Bract. A small, modified leaf. The scalelike leaves come in a flower cluster. Some bracts, such as dogwood, are large and showy.

Cluster Plantings. Grouping at least three to five plants of one variety together to make a strong visual statement. Odd numbers grouped together tend to be more appealing to the eye than even numbers.

Corm. The fleshy underground stem from which crocuses and gladiolus grow. Corms are often mistakenly called bulbs.

Cultivar. A named variety of a plant that has been produced under controlled conditions by plant breeders. Short for "cultivated variety."

Division. Digging up a clump of perennials, breaking into smaller segments, and replanting the segments. Division is done to control the size of the perennial clump, to rejuvenate an old plant, or to propagate new plants.

Drifts. Five or more plants of the same type (and usually the same color) planted in an irregular pattern (as opposed to a straight row), making a wave of color in an informal planting such as in a cottage garden.

Hardy. Plants which live and thrive in a given climate, capable of enduring the climate's coldest temperatures. Hardy perennials die to the ground in winter, but the roots remain alive and send up new growth each year.

Mass Plantings. An area or bed planted in all one variety and color of plant, such as mass planting of red tulips.

Old Wood. Growth from the previous season. Some types of clematis bloom on "old wood," or growth from last year. If pruned to the ground, as one should do with the vari-

eties that bloom on this year's growth ("new wood), no blooms would occur.

Panicle. A loose, spirelike arrangement of flowers on a stalk, such as lilacs.

Perennial. A plant that dies back during winter months and comes back every spring. Perennials tend to have shorter blooming periods than annuals.

Root Bound. A term used for a potted plant indicating that the roots fill the pot with little or no excess soil between the roots and the edge of the pot. Some plants, such as geraniums, bloom more profusely when root bound.

Setting Seed. The time in the bloom cycle at which the flower begins to fade and seed formation occurs.

Solid Beds. A flower bed planted in all one variety of a plant, such as a solid bed of marigolds.

Succulent. A descriptive term referring to the fleshiness and amount of moisture contained in a bloom or stem. Some blooms, such as hyacinth, are too succulent to press well.

Tuberous Roots. (Also known as tubers.) Swollen underground stems filled with reserved food and having buds or eyes from which the plant grows. The tuber's food supply supports the plant until feeding roots develop. Dahlias have tuberous roots.

Zone. Established by the U.S. Department of Agriculture, zones are breakdowns of climate giving the annual minimum temperature range for each zone.

Approximate Ranges

Zone 1	Below -50°F
Zone 2	-50 to -40°F
Zone 3	-40 to -30°F
Zone 4	-30 to -20°F
Zone 5	-20 to -10°F
Zone 6	-10 to 0°F
Zone 7	0 to 10°F
Zone 8	10 to 20°F
Zone 9	20 to 30°F
Zone 10	30 to 40°F

Flower Profiles

American Bittersweet
CELASTRUS SCANDENS

Native to America, this fast-growing, woody vine produces bright yellow berries in the fall and can grow to 20' (6.6 m) if not kept under control with yearly trimmings. When fully ripe, the berries split open to reveal a crimson seed.

Growing and Landscaping

Bittersweet will grow in sun or shade and is not particular about its soil conditions. When purchasing bittersweet, be sure to get both a male and female or berries will not be produced. Hardy to zone 4.

Bittersweet looks especially pretty on a low wall, trellis or post, and makes a beautiful display rambling over banks and slopes.

Harvesting and Drying

Harvest the berries in the fall after they have split open. Hang the stems upside down to dry or dry them upright. Do not microwave the berries — they explode into a large mess.

Crafting

Bittersweet vines make excellent wreath bases. Shape the fresh-cut vines into a wreath form, secure with floral wire, and allow to dry. Use the berries in arrangements, wreaths, or alone in a vase for a bright crimson display. The berries make wonderful accents in winter holiday projects.

Annual Statice
LIMONIUM SINUATUM

One of the easiest annuals to grow and dry, the graceful sprays of statice floriets seem to float on its dark green foliage. Statice averages 12 to 30" (30 to 75 cm) and comes in a variety of bright colors, including blue, lavender, purple, red, pink, yellow, and white.

Growing and Landscaping
With its abundance of florist-quality flowers in brilliant colors, annual statice deserves usage in gardens. Scatter statice amid other plants in the perennial garden to add season-long color where other perennials have ceased their blooming period. Plant low-growing varieties in rock gardens or in containers with other colorful annuals such as marigolds and geraniums, or plant a row of statice in the cutting garden.

Annual statice needs a well-drained soil and full sun, but it will tolerate heat, drought, and low fertility. Space the plants 12 to 24" (30 to 60 cm) apart and water only if conditions are very dry.

Harvesting and Drying
Harvest the blooms when they are fully opened. (Picking the blossoms encourages abundant reblooming.) Hang small bundles of blooms upside down to dry or dry single stems on a screen rack.

Because of the feathery quality of individual petals, annual statice dries well enough to just put it in a fresh bouquet with other blooms; by the time the other blooms have lost their fresh-cut look, the statice will probably be dry. The blooms can also be dried in the microwave for two minutes at a medium setting, but it's hardly worth the effort because of the ease of air-drying. The blooms retain virtually all of their bright color and interesting shape with very little shrinkage.

Crafting
Annual statice is a popular choice for virtually all floral crafts because of its bright colors (a good source of purple!) and the curving nature of its sprays. For use in small projects, break the sprays down into smaller segments.

Aster
ASTER

Aster's daisylike flowers bloom in large clusters in late summer and fall. The yellow centers have petals ranging in color from deep purple through lavender, blue, pink, rose, and white, often with 2" (5 cm) diameters.

Growing and Landscaping

Asters provide excellent color in the late summer and fall. The dwarf varieties (6", 15 cm) are good for borders and as rock garden accents. The tall varieties (6', 1.8 m) work well in the back of the border, especially when planted in groups of three. The intermediate varieties are good to intersperse in the perennial border to add color in late summer when most other perennials have ceased blooming.

Propagate the plants by division in the spring, and plant them 12 to 18" (30 to 46 cm) apart in full to partial sun in average, well-drained soil. Pinch back in the late spring for added bushiness. The tall varieties need staking. Hardy to zone 4.

Harvesting and Drying

Asters can be air-dried on a screen rack or hung upside down in small bunches. The petals tend to curl as they dry, darken by several shades, and shrink substantially. Harvest the blooms before they are fully open. (Flowers harvested later in the bloom cycle fall apart.) Asters can also be dried in the microwave for two minutes on a medium setting; the petals brown slightly, although the interesting curls may make you overlook the browning. For perfect color and shape retention, dry the blooms in a desiccant.

Crafting

Because they shrink so much during the drying process, asters are best used in clusters as colorful background materials. They look especially lovely in harvest wreaths, with strawflowers and/or globe amaranths as focal flowers. Dried asters are an excellent source for natural shades of blue.

Astilbe

ASTILBE

Known commonly as perennial spirea and false spirea, this strong, herbaceous perennial grows from 1 to 2' (.3 to .6 m) in height and bears 12 to 18" (30 to 46 cm) feathery plumes in white, pink, lavender, and red in early summer.

Growing and Landscaping

Astilbe prefers a rich, moist soil and partial shade, although it will do well in deep shade and will also accept full sun if it is watered frequently. Space the plants 12 to 18" apart. Astilbe needs a good organic fertilizing just as growth begins each spring. Hardy to zone 4.

Astilbe's lush, fernlike foliage is attractive from spring to frost, and it makes an attractive drift in a woodland or shade garden and also adds grace to a perennial border.

Harvesting and Drying

Astilbe plumes can be harvested at any time. For autumn wreaths and arrangements, harvest them after they've browned. Air-dry the blooms on a screen or upside down; expect the colors to darken several shades and slight shrinkage to occur. Air-dry astilbe plumes upright if you want arching plumes.

Astilbe can be dried in the microwave for two to three minutes on a medium setting, but several of the shades turn brown. Astilbe is suitable for pressing.

Crafting

Dried astilbe blooms can be used as backgrounds in arrangements, wreaths, sprays, swags…anywhere a graceful, feathery effect is desired. Astilbe can also be spraypainted with floral paint or gold enamel to achieve a wider color range. The plumes can be cut into smaller segments and attached with floral picks. Pressed astilbe makes a nice background for pressed flower arrangements.

Baby's Breath
GYPSOPHILA PANICULATA

This well-known perennial produces cloudlike mists of tiny white or pink flowers. The blooms come in massive quantities on sturdy, well-branched stalks, creating an airy, delicate effect. The named cultivars have usually been grafted and are superior enough to warrant a trip to a garden center.

Growing and Landscaping
Plant baby's breath in the spring in full sun and well-drained soil. Since they may reach 3' (.9 m) tall and possibly as wide, be sure to space them at least 2' (.6 m) apart. Keep the flowers picked before they set seed to prolong the blooming season. Baby's breath does not transplant well. Hardy to zone 3.

Baby's breath makes a lovely focal point in a perennial border, as well as in rock gardens and cutting gardens.

Harvesting and Drying
Harvest baby's breath when the flowers have just opened, before they have begun to discolor or set seed. Hang them upside down in small bunches to air-dry, or dry them upright in a waterless vase. Expect good size and color rentention. Microwaving for three to four minutes on a medium setting produces similar results but is hardly worth the effort given how receptive the blooms are to air drying.

Crafting
Baby's breath makes a lovely filler material in spring and bridal wreaths, tussie mussies, and arrangements. For smaller projects, break the stems down into smaller segments. Dried baby's breath can be custom-matched to any decor with a floral spray colorant.

Bachelor Buttons
CENTAUREA CYANUS

This old-fashioned annual averages 12 to 16" (30 to 41 cm) and comes in shades of blue, violet, pink, and white.

Growing and Landscaping
Bachelor buttons will tolerate poor soil and should be spaced 6 to 12" (15 to 30 cm) apart. The taller varieties may need staking and the blooms tend to decline in late summer and are best simply removed from the garden and replaced, perhaps with chrysanthemums. Bachelor buttons look lovely in annual beds, perennial beds, and borders, and also in the cutting garden.

Harvesting and Drying
Bachelor buttons are best dried in silica gel when the blooms are just fully open. Wire the flower heads for support before drying. Expect little shrinkage and good color retention; the blue shades tend to darken a bit.

Crafting
Choose bachelor buttons for floral crafts where a blue accent is desired. Bachelor buttons add a nice touch to harvest wreaths of multicolored blooms and to tussie mussies and nosegays. They are good sources for natural shades of blue.

Bee Balm
MONARDA DIDYMA

A member of the mint family, this 2 to 3' (.6 to .9 m) perennial does well in the north but it can be invasive in southern gardens. Bee balm's vigorous, bushy stem clusters bear flowers in shades of pink, purple, white, and red, and their spicy scents attract butterflies, bees, and hummingbirds.

Growing and Landscaping
Plant bee balm in full sun and space 12 to 24" (30 to 60 cm) apart. Water well for best appearance but withhold fertilizer to prevent rapid spreading. Bee balm is easily increased by division every three years. Bee balm is ideal in herb gardens, butterfly gardens, sunny wild gardens, and in bold groups in the perennial border. Hardy to zone 4.

Harvesting and Drying
Harvest bee balm when it's in full bloom. Air-dry by hanging in bunches of five or six. The blooms retain their size and shape well with a slight darkening in color. The foliage curls and becomes rather brittle but retains its minty aroma. Bee balm can be microwaved with good success. Arrange the blooms on a paper towel and dry for two minutes at a medium setting. Bee balm does not press well.

Crafting
Bee balm's bright colors and multipetaled blooms are lovely in herbal garlands, wreaths, potpourris, and arrangements.

Black-Eyed Susan
RUDBECKIA FULGIDA

Native of eastern North America, perennial black-eyed Susans are treasured in the garden because of their deep yellow blooms and lush, dense foliage. The 2-1/2' (.75 m) plants need little attention and bloom from mid-July until frost.

Growing and Landscaping

Ideally, black-eyed Susans should be planted in well-drained soil in full sun with 12 to 18" (30 to 46 cm) spacing. The plants will also survive in light shade, but they will have fewer blooms and a more leggy appearance. Divide the plants every five years to maintain vigor. Hardy to zone 4. Black-eyed Susans are an excellent choice for perennial borders to add bright, mid- to late-season color. For maximum effect, plant them in drifts. Black-eyed Susans look nice in rock gardens, cutting gardens, and even in the vegetable garden for fall color.

Harvesting and Drying

Harvest the plants when their blooms have just fully opened, double checking to make sure they are not damp. Dry them upside down in small bunches or on a screen. The petals will curl a little and shrink to half of their fresh-cut size, but they are still attractive. The stems remain strong and sturdy.

For microwave drying, choose the smaller, younger blooms, cut the stems close, and microwave on a medium setting for two to three minutes. The blooms will shrink about 30% and wrinkle some, but the colors stay bright. Desiccant drying gives almost perfect shape and color retention. The blooms are too thick for pressing.

Crafting

With their yellow petals and central black cone, black-eyed Susans make wonderful additions to fall wreaths and arrangements. The central seed cone (petals removed) looks nice in harvest arrangements.

Candytuft
IBERIS UMBELLATA

Native to Southern Europe and Japan, this 12 to 18" (30 to 46 cm) annual produces a carpet of color in a tumbling, mounded pattern. Masses of unscented flowers bloom in rose, lavender, mauve, and white from June through frost.

Growing and Landscaping

Plant in well-drained soils in full sun. Candytuft tolerates drought, heat, and dry soils, but it does not do well in regions of cool summers. Remove the flowers as they fade to prolong the plant's blooming cycle. If planted in a formal garden, candytuft should be sheared frequently to maintain tidiness.

Candytuft is a particularly good choice for use in more informal, natural settings. It creates beautiful carpets of color, and is pretty tucked between rocks or a in wall, or on a difficult, stony slope. Candytuft also works well as an edging plant in borders and in solid beds.

Harvesting and Drying

Harvest at the peak of bloom when the flowers have just fully opened. Air-dry on a screen to keep the bloom clusters from drooping. Shrinkage will be about 40% but the colors stay well. Candytuft dries very well in the microwave. Arrange the blooms on a paper towel and microwave for three to five minutes on a medium setting. Candytuft can also be dried in a desiccant with far less shrinkage, or it can be pressed.

Crafting

Clusters of dried candytuft are attractive for use in smaller wreaths, tussie mussies, and virtually anywhere a dainty look is desired. The individual florets add nice color to potpourris.

Carnation

DIANTHUS CARYOPHYLLUS
AND DIANTHUS HYBRIDS (COTTAGE PINKS)

This tender, 2 to 3-1/2' (.6 to 1.1 m) perennial has been cultivated for more than twenty centuries, and the name carnation comes from its use in garlands and coronets in ancient Greece. The ruffled flowers come in shades of red, white, and pink.

Growing and Landscaping

Perennial dianthus should be planted in full sun in a rich, well-drained soil. They do not do well in areas with hot, muggy summers. Use carnations as an edging or border plant where the mat of foliage can freely spread. Hardy to zone 3.

Harvesting and Drying

Harvest the blooms at their peak when they are just fully open. Air-dry the blooms on a screen and wire the stems while they are fresh-cut if you plan to use them in an arrangement; the petals will curl some but the colors stay vibrant. Carnations will also dry well upright in a vase of water.

The blooms can be microwaved on a medium setting for four to five minutes with substantial shrinkage and color changing. The foliage and blooms of some hybrids can be pressed, but most nonhybrids are too succulent to press well.

Crafting

Carnation blooms are welcome additions to wreaths, garlands, swags, arrangements, and baskets.

Chrysanthemum

CHRYSANTHEMUM HYBRIDS

More than 150 species of this plant are grown, providing a sensational fall color display. Most varieties are fully double flowering, with blooms in all colors except blue. Plant heights range from 1 to 4' (.3 to 1.2 m) with attractive, dark green foliage. Plant shapes vary from low, mound-shaped cushion mums to tall, narrow upright types.

Growing and Landscaping

Well-drained soil is critical if chrysanthemums are to survive the winter. They will bloom best in full sun, although they will accept partial shade. From spring until mid-July, pinch the tips of the plants to encourage bushier foliage and more abundant blooming. Tall plants may need staking, and all varieties need to be fertilized and watered well throughout the growing season. Divide annually to propagate and rejuvenate the plants. Hardy in zones 5 through 9; zone 5 needs mulching.

Use chrysanthemums in perennial borders to add fall color when most other perennials have ceased blooming. The dwarf varieties work well in the front of beds and borders. Chrysanthemums also look nice in container plantings on decks and patios.

Harvesting and Drying

Harvest the blooms when they are fully open and at their peak, double-checking to make sure they are not damp to prevent browning. Most varieties will dry well with desiccants, retaining their color, size, and form. Some varieties will dry well on a screen with some petal curling, color darkening, and about 30% shrinkage. Some varieties will also air-dry upright. If you plan to use them in an arrangement, wire the fresh-cut stems.

Microwave drying for five to six minutes on a medium setting produces good results if you don't mind a 50% size shrinkage. The leaves curl but the stems remain sturdy. Chrysanthemums are not suitable for pressing.

Crafting

Chrysanthemums are good additions to fall harvest wreaths and arrangements, while the colorful petals look nice in potpourris.

Clematis
CLEMATIS

This woody climbing vine makes a welcome addition to home gardens. It features large, showy flowers in shades of white, pink, red, blue, lavender, and purple and spiked seed pods in the fall.

Growing and Landscaping

There are many species (and also many hybrids) of clematis with varying habits and flower forms. Some varieties flower from the old wood and should be pruned only to remove straggly, weak, or undesired shoots when dormant. Other varieties flower from young basal shoots and should have all the growth cut back in the spring. Be sure to investigate the needs of your specific plant.

Clematis thrives in fertile, well-dug soil. The plants themselves like sun, but the roots need to be kept cool. Mulch the roots and plant day lilies or hostas around the roots to provide shade. Fertilize frequently with a water-soluble fertilizer. Zones 3 through 9.

Harvesting and Drying

Mature blossoms may be dried in a desiccant with fairly good results. (They darken, curl, and shrink substantially during air- drying and turn brown in the microwave.) The viny stems and wispy, spiked seed heads are the plant's main attractions to crafters. Hang the seed heads upside down to dry.

Crafting

The seed heads are inviting additions to autumn wreaths and arrangements. Unique wreath bases can be formed by wrapping a circle of vines (with seed heads attached) into a wreath base. The vines also make wonderful garland bases for decorating mantels, doorways, or large basket handles.

Common Immortelle
XERANTHEMUM

One of the oldest cultivated "everlastings," common immortelle averages 1-1/2 to 2' (.45 to .6 m) tall and is grown primarily for its papery flowers. The satiny-textured blooms come in shades of white, pink, rose, violet, and purple. Some varieties have semi-double or double flowers.

Growing and Landscaping
Plant in full sun in average soil; the plants tolerate heat well. Common immortelle is best reserved for the cutting garden since the plant itself is not especially attractive. Harvesting is easier if they are planted together in rows or groups. Pick the flowers often for abundant reblooming.

Harvesting and Drying
Harvest when the blooms are fully open and air-dry by hanging upside down in small bunches. Expect good retention of color, shape, and size. Because of the papery texture of the blooms, they are almost dry when harvested, so desiccant or microwave drying isn't worth the effort. The blooms press well.

Crafting
The blooms are wonderful in any craft needing small, delicate accent flowers. Use them in clusters for maximum effect. Their satiny textures make them a nice choice for corsages and tree ornaments.

Coneflower
ECHINACEA

Native to North American prairies and meadows, this 3 to 5' (.9 to 1.5 m) drought-resistant, daisy-like flower has petals that radiate downward from a conical, bristly seed head. The showy flowers range in color from white to pink to deep purple, and bloom from July through September. The coneflower's botanical name, Echinacea, comes from the Greek word for hedgehog, suggested by the bristly seed heads.

Growing and Landscaping

Coneflowers prefer sandy, well-drained soil in full sun or light shade. They should be spaced 18 to 24" (46 to 60 cm) apart and divided every three to four years to rejuvenate the plants. Hardy to zones 3 through 9. Coneflowers are great for use in perennial borders, English cottage gardens, butterfly gardens, and cutting gardens. The stiff, tall stems require no staking, and the seed heads remain attractive in the garden even after the flowers fade.

Harvesting and Drying

Harvest the flowers when they are in full bloom. Hang dry them upside down in small bunches or arrange them on a screen. The petals will shrink about 50% and curl slightly. The seed heads can be harvested late in the season, after the petals have fallen off, and dried by hanging. The heads will dry to an attractive, brownish-maroon color. Desiccant drying in silica gel ensures a more perfect appearance with less shrinkage and much less petal curling. The stems remain sturdy.

Younger blooms can be dried in the microwave for two to three minutes on medium power. If they are still not dry in the center, finish drying them with one of the air-drying techniques. (Further microwaving will cause the petals to brown.) Coneflowers do not press well.

Crafting

Coneflower blooms make nice additions to wreaths and arrangements that need bright color. Their curling petals are especially attractive in harvest wreaths that are densely packed with many types of flowers. Silica-dried blooms make good accent flowers against greenery backgrounds.

The naturally dark seed heads look nice in autumn crafts. They can be sprayed with a light coat of gold to create wonderful accents in Christmas wreaths, arrangements, swags, and garlands.

Coreopsis
COREOPSIS LANCEOLATA

A member of the daisy family, this perennial herb, ranging in height from 1 to 2' (.3 to .6 m), blooms with golden yellow daisylike flowers or semidouble blooms and bears flowers from June through frost.

Growing and Landscaping

Long-lived coreopsis will spread slowly. Space the plants 12 to 18" (30 to 46 cm) apart and propagate by root division in early spring. Removing spent blooms extends the blooming season. Coreopsis is extremely tolerant to most growing conditions, although it shows a preference for full sun and well-drained soils. Hardy to zone 3.

Because of its extremely long bloom season, coreopsis is a wonderful addition to the perennial garden, in sunny English cottage gardens, rock gardens, cutting gardens, and as colorful accents in herb gardens. Arrange the plants in drifts of at least three for the best effect, and plant them near perennials with shorter blooming seasons.

Harvesting and Drying

Harvest the blooms when they are fully opened, then hang upside down in small bundles. The blooms will shrink by about 50% and darken in color to a deep gold. If you'd prefer the petals to remain fully open, air-dry the blooms on a screen. The stems remain sturdy and can be picked directly into floral foam.

The blooms can also be microwaved for two minutes on a medium setting with results similar to air-drying, or they can be dried in a desiccant for near-perfect retention of shape and color. Harvest the seed pods later in the season; hang them upside down to dry and tie a cheesecloth bag around the pods to catch the seeds.

Crafting

Coreopsis blooms are an excellent choice for harvest wreaths or in any project needing a colorful, golden-yellow accent. The dried seed pods can be sprayed gold or other colors for pretty accents in floral crafts.

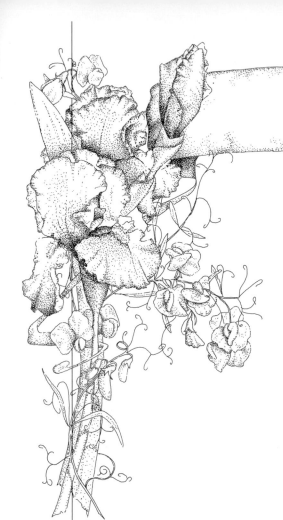

Crested Cockscomb
CELOSIA CRISTATA

Native to Africa, this stunning, 6 to 12" (15 to 30 cm) annual has tightly borne, convoluted flowers resembling a rooster's comb. they bloom from June through October in shades of bright yellow, orange, red, pink, and purple.

Growing and Landscaping

Cockscomb likes full sun and 6 to 12" spacing in a rich, well-drained soil high in organic matter. Water moderately during dry spells. Crested cockscomb is best used as an unusual accent at the front of the border. It can also be used as an edging plant or in a container planting mixed with other annuals.

Harvesting and Drying

Harvest the blooms at their peak, double-checking to be sure there is no dampness on the blooms, and air-dry by hanging or on a screen for excellent retention of size, color, and form. The blooms are too thick for pressing; microwave and desiccant drying are hardly worth the effort when air-drying yields such lovely results.

Crafting

Crested celosia blooms make lovely accents in large wreaths. For smaller projects, break the blooms down into smaller segments. Their brilliant colors and interesting textures make them great to work with.

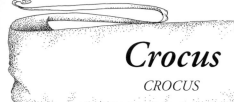

Crocus
CROCUS

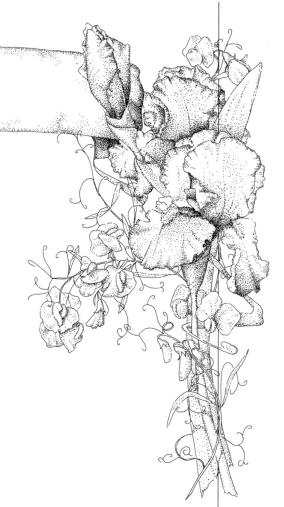

This genus of the iris family blooms in very early spring, sometimes when snow is still on the ground in the North. The blooms come in brilliant colors of yellow, purple, lavender, and white.

Growing and Landscaping
Plant the corms in the fall, fertilize well, and leave them in the ground to multiply. Propagate in mid-summer by digging them up and separating them, then replanting 3" (7.5 cm) deep and 3" apart.

Mass crocus plantings are the most spectacular. Use them in perennial beds, rock gardens, in front of shrubbery, and scattered in the lawn since they will bloom before the grass needs mowing.

Harvesting and Drying
Harvest the blooms when they have just opened, double-checking to be sure the flowers are not damp. Air-dry the blooms upside down, but expect the buds to close and shrink about 50%. For best retention of color and form, dry them in a desiccant. Some luck may be had with pressing.

Crafting
Crocuses make bright, colorful accents to spring wreaths, hats, arrangements, and any type of Easter display. They look great combined with pussy willows and daffodils.

Daffodil
NARCISSUS

This genus of spring-flowering bulbs is characterized by white, yellow, and orange flowers.

Growing and Landscaping

Daffodils are planted in the fall and bloom the following spring. Next year's buds form as the foliage dries, so do not disturb the foliage as it dries down. Propagate daffodils by lifting the bulbs after the foliage has withered. Separate the bulbs and replant them immediately for best results, then fertilize well with an organic fertilizer.

Daffodil clumps will enlarge over the years, so they are good choices for naturalizing areas such as woodland gardens, rock gardens, slopes, and perennial gardens. They are most effectively planted in mass where they can make a large display.

Harvesting and Drying

Harvest the blooms when they are partially open for dried buds or when they have just fully opened for full blossoms. The yellow daffodils will air-dry by hanging or upright drying in a vase. Expect some shrinkage and some deepening in color. The white varieties are best dried in a desiccant.

Crafting

Daffodils bring a sunny accent to any floral craft. They work especially well in combination with pussy willows and crocus.

Dahlia

DAHLIA

These large, showy flowers come in virtually every color except blue and bloom from July through frost.

Growing and Landscaping

Averaging 12 to 24" (30 to 60 cm), dahlias look lovely in cutting gardens, perennial borders, and in large containers on a deck or patio. Plant the tuberous roots in a fertile (high in organic matter) soil with 18 to 36" (46 to 92 cm) spacing in the spring after all chance of frost, then dig them up in late fall and store in a cool, dark place until it's time to replant. Fertilize the plants monthly for maximum blooms; the tall varieties may need staking.

Harvesting and Drying

Dahlias should be harvested after their blooms have fully opened, taking care that there is no moisture in the dense petals. Dahlias dry well by hanging upside down in groups of three. They shrink about 30% and their colors darken some. (White dahlias, for example, dry to a creamy ivory.) Dahlias can also be dried on a screen, with or without their stems, depending on the gauge of your screen mesh.

Dahlias can be microwaved for five to six minutes on a medium power setting. The dense center areas will still be damp and should be hung upside down to finish air-drying. Another drying option is to place the fresh-cut flowers in a water-filled vase; as the water evaporates from the container, the blooms dry in an upright position. Pressing does not work well because the blooms are too thick.

Crafting

The large blooms are real attention-getters in harvest wreaths, swags, and just about anywhere else that needs a large focal flower. If you plan to use the dried blooms in an arrangement, wire the stems before drying.

Delphinium
DELPHINIUM

This classically elegant perennial features tall flower spires, primarily in rich blue, but also in pink, white, and purple. Semi-dwarf varieties range from 2-1/2 to 3' (.7 to .9 m), while the taller, standard varieties can be more than 5' (1.5 m) and will need to be staked. The dense flowers bloom in June and July on tall spikes.

Growing and Landscaping
Plant delphiniums in rich, well-drained soil in full sun. A native of the cool, mountainous regions of Europe, delphiniums will decline in areas with hot, muggy summers. Propagate by division in early spring, and fertilize and water well. A second crop of blooms can sometimes be produced by cutting back the plant after the first blooming cycle. Hardy to zone 2.

For a striking effect, use the taller varieties at the back of the perennial border in groups of three or more. Semidwarf varieties are attractive in the middle of the border for vertical accents.

Harvesting and Drying
Harvest when the blooms are at their peak or when the top florets are still in bud form. Air-dry the blooms upside down with lots of space in between to keep the circulation good and prevent crushing. Expect some shrinkage and good color retention. Microwave drying for four to five minutes on a medium setting yields similar results. Desiccant drying gives more perfect shape and color retention. Individual blooms press well.

Crafting
Use delphinium whenever long spikes of rich color and a strong vertical look is desired. They look nice in wreaths and arrangements and also make lovely bases for swags.

Dogwood
CORNUS FLORIDA

This small, ornamental tree ranges up to 30' (10 m) high and features lovely spring blooms. The graceful, horizontal branches form dark green summer foliage which turns to purplish red in the fall. The birds enjoy the tree's fall berries.

Growing and Landscaping

Flowering dogwoods thrive in well-drained soil in partial shade or full sun; they can not survive in poorly drained soil or drought conditions. The spring flowers are actually pink and white, four-petaled bracts and they appear before the leaves. Hardy to zone 5. (The white is more hardy.)

Dogwoods are beautiful wherever they are used, in groups or as a single specimen. Their small size makes them a good choice for near the house or patio, and they also look nice in woodland shade gardens under a canopy of full-size deciduous trees or as a specimen plant in an island in the lawn.

Harvesting and Drying

Harvest dogwood bracts at the peak of their blooming. Entire branches my be cut and hung to dry or the individual bracts may be picked and dried on a screen. Be sure they have not gone past their peak or they will turn brown. The petals will shrink about 30% and curl slightly, but the effect is lovely. For most perfect retention of color and form, use a desiccant. The leaves and bracts also press well.

Crafting

Dogwoods look lovely in spring wreaths, especially in combination with spring daffodils and crocus, with pussy willows, or as a single accent on pussy willow wreaths and swags.

Feverfew
CHRYSANTHEMUM PARTHENIUM

This perennial, old-time garden favorite is a member of the daisy family and native to southeastern Europe. The tiny, daisylike flowers (white with yellow centers) bloom in profusion on low, bushy plants from July through frost. The single varieties self-sow almost invasively, while the double varieties are a little less vigorous.

Growing and Landscaping
Feverfew averages 12 to 15" (30 to 39 cm) in height and does best in sandy, well-drained soils with full sun to partial shade. Space the plants 12 to 14" (30 to 36 cm) apart, and pinch or shear them early in the season to retain bushiness. Propagate by replanting the self-sown seedlings or by division in the spring. Feverfew is a great choice for borders, cutting gardens, English cottage gardens, and herb gardens. Hardy to zone 4.

Harvesting and Drying
Harvest any time during the blooming cycle and hang upside down in small bundles. The blossoms darken to a creamy color as they dry with some shrinking and curling. The foliage curls also but retains its light green color. Microwave drying produces an unacceptable amount of browning and curling. Both the flowers and leaves press well. For perfect retention of shape and color, dry short stems in silica gel.

Crafting
Clusters of feverfew add a delicate look to wreaths, hats, swags, and garlands. The tiny flowers lend themselves well to small-scale decorations such as picture frames, birdhouses, Christmas ornaments, potpourris, and miniature baskets.

Foxglove
DIGITALIS

Several varieties of foxglove are popular garden plants. Two of the varieties, digitalis lantana and digitalis mertonensis, are true perennials, while Digitalis purpurea is actually a biennial that reseeds itself. The tubular, 2-1/2" (7 cm) flowers are borne on tall spikes in June and July in shades of purple, pink, white, red, and yellow. Foxgloves grow 2 to 5' (.6 to 1.5 m) tall, with large dark green wrinkled leaves.

Growing and Landscaping

Foxglove's tall spikes of color lend a spectacular vertical effect to gardens. The plants prefer shade but will tolerate full sun. Plant in moist, well-drained soil spaced 18 to 24" (46 to 60 cm) apart and propagate them by division every two years. Zones 4 through 8.

Foxgloves look spectacular planted in the rear of the perennial border in clumps of three. Foxgloves also make nice additions to woodland shade gardens or in a row along a garden fence.

Harvesting and Drying

Harvest the flowers any time — from buds to full bloom — for a variety of shapes. Double-check for dampness to prevent browning. For best retention of color and shape, remove the individual flowers from the spire and dry them in a desiccant. The individual blooms can also be pressed with pleasant results. Microwaving for six minutes on a medium setting flattens the blooms and browns them slightly around the edges. The stems become firm and durable.

Crafting

Foxglove spires are cherished in craft projects because of their unusual shape. Consider clustering them in groups of three for stunning effects. Because the stems do not wire well, air-dried blooms will need to be secured in place with glue or floral pins.

Geraniums
PELARGONIUM XHORTORUM

This tender perennial averages 12 to 24" (30 to 60 cm) in height and is usually grown as an annual. Its long blooming season (from May through frost) produces blooms in red, pink, salmon, orange, and white.

Growing and Landscaping

Geraniums prefer full sun and a rich soil that is high in organic matter. Space them 8 to 18" (20 to 46 cm) apart, depending on the variety, and give them liberal waterings and weekly feedings with a water-soluble fertilizer. Cut the plant back if it begins to get spindly, and pinch off any spent blooms for abundant blossoming. Geraniums propagated from stem cuttings root easily, while some of the newer varieties can be started from seed.

Geraniums are excellent to use in mass plantings, in borders, hanging baskets, and window boxes. If grown in pots, they prefer to be root-bound.

Harvesting and Drying

To dry in the microwave, arrange single blooms face down and microwave for five to six minutes on medium power. Expect some loss in shape and good color retention. The leaves shrink to about half their fresh-cut size and darken in color.

To air-dry geraniums, break the flower clusters into individual florets and dry them on a screen, or hang them upside down in small bundles just until dry. Expect the size and form to change considerably during the drying process. For good shape and color retention, dry in a desiccant or by pressing, checking frequently to make sure they do not overdry.

Crafting

Geranium petals add nice color to potpourri, while the foliage of the scented varieties contributes a pleasant fragrance. The dainty flowers work well in smaller wreaths. The pressed blooms add a beautiful look to pressed flower pictures, bookmarks, and stationery.

German Statice
LIMONIUM DUMOSUM

This lovely perennial features heads of silvery-white flowers that form a canopy over green foliage with red undersides. Heights range from 14" to 3' (36 cm to .9 m), depending on variety.

Growing and Landscaping

Plant German statice in full sun in any type of soil with 12 to 18" spacing (30 to 46 cm). Propagate by division in the spring. Hardy to zone 5.

German statice looks lovely in rock gardens, cutting gardens, or in the midst of the perennial garden for a light, airy touch. German statice is a nice choice in the perennial garden to fill in where early perennials, such as Oriental poppies, have ceased blooming and died back.

Harvesting and Drying

Harvest German statice when the flowers are fully open. The blooms air-dry easily with little loss in color or size because of their papery texture. The dried stems are sturdy enough to pick directly into wreath bases or floral foam. Given the ease and quality of air-drying, microwave and desiccant techniques are not worth the effort. German statice does not press well.

Crafting

German statice adds volume, shape, and delicate beauty to arrangements and wreaths, and can be used either as an accent or background material. Stems of German statice can be broken into smaller segments for use in smaller projects, and these shorter stems have a graceful, curving look to them.

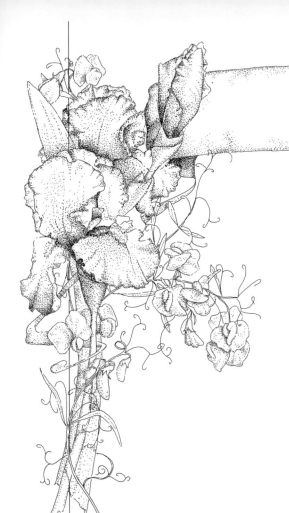

Globe Amaranth
GOMPHRENA GLOBOSA

This annual everlasting blooms in pinks, whites, oranges, creams, lavenders, and purples. Native to the eastern tropics, globe amaranth ranges in height from 9 to 30" (22 to 75 cm), and its papery, cloverlike blossoms have a long blooming season.

Growing and Landscaping
Plant in light, well-drained soil in full sun with 10 to 15" spacing. Globes easily survive neglect, heat, drought, and poor soil conditions; avoid overwatering. The tall standards (up to 30") are best reserved for the cutting garden, while the dwarf varieties are good for edgings, borders, cottage gardens, and to add color in herb gardens.

Harvesting and Drying
Harvest only when the flowers are very mature, toward the end of the summer, leaving the leaves on the stems if desired. The blooms air-dry easily by hanging upside down, retaining their color and shapes very well. Dry the blooms upright if you prefer a curving stem. Microwave drying is not worth the effort since air-drying produces such good results.

Crafting
These colorful everlastings have virtually unlimited craft usage. Some of the smaller flowers are great for tree ornaments, miniature baskets, and dollhouse accessories. They look lovely in wreaths when clustered in bunches of three to five. The magenta globes look wonderful tucked into miniature Christmas trees. The softer cream and mauve colors are good for Victorian-style decorating.

Heather
CALLUNA VULGARIS

Native to Europe and Asia, this perennial grows in compact, 2' (.6 m) tall clumps with rosy-pink flowers blooming in late fall. Heath (Erica) is often confused with heather. They are both members of the same family but heathers are hardier and will survive in northern gardens.

Growing and Landscaping

Heathers should be planted in full sun or partial shade in fertile, acid soil, preferably with peat moss added. Fertilize with a water- soluble acid fertilizer. Shear the plants in the spring to keep them compact and blooming profusely. Plant several heathers together for pleasing drifts of color and foliage, or plant as an edging plant in the perennial border. Hardy to zone 5.

Harvesting and Drying

Pick the blooms just as they begin to dry naturally on the plant and air-dry them upright in a container with a little water; as the water evaporates, the flowers dry, producing a less brittle flower with good shape and color retention. Heather blooms press well.

Crafting

Heather makes a wonderful accent material in wreaths, baskets, arrangments, swags, and decorative birdhouses. If the blooms are shredding as you work with them, spritz them with a mixture of 1/2 teaspoon of fabric softener and 1 quart of water.

Hollyhock
ALCEA ROSEA

A favorite since Shakespearian times, hollyhock's stately spires of double-ruffled flowers bloom from June through September and come in shades of red, white, pink, and maroon.

Growing and Landscaping

Plant in full sun in well-drained soil about 2' apart. Water and feed heavily. The taller varieties (up to 9', 3 m) may require staking to protect them from rain and wind, but their tremendous display is well worth the effort.

Hollyhocks are ideal in the back of the border. Plant the dwarf varieties (2', .6 m) in the middle of the perennial border for a strong textural accent. Hollyhock is a mainstay in cottage gardens.

Harvesting and Drying

Remove the blossoms from the spires and dry them individually on an air screen. Expect about 40% shrinkage; the blossoms will close slightly and the petals will curl a little, but the color retention is very good. For best retention of color and form, dry in a desiccant. Hollyhock is too large for pressing.

Crafting

Dried hollyhock blooms look like a small peony, and they work well with projects using many different types of flowers. Blooms will need to be hot-glued in place since the weak stems do not wire well.

Honeysuckle

LONICERA HENRYI OR
LONICERA JAPONICA "HALLIANA"

Native to Japan and China, Lonicera henryi's twining vines are blessed with sweet-smelling flowers that bloom from June through August in colors from yellow to purplish red. Japonica is a more rampant variety with dense, dark green foliage and deliciously fragrant, creamy white flowers that bloom from spring through frost. Both varieties thrive in full sun or partial shade and tolerate any soil except wet areas.

Growing and Landscaping

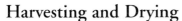

Honeysuckle's excellent root system holds well on steep banks to form a rambling ground cover. Lonicera japonica can get out of control and smother trees and shrubs if not contained by pruning. Both varieties are good for covering a fence, bank or other barrier. Cut it back ruthlessly if it threatens to outgrow its intended area. Hardy to zone 5.

Harvesting and Drying

Harvest honeysuckle blossoms when they are at their peak and air-dry on a screen or by pressing. The blooms turn brown in the microwave unless watched with great care; prepare to ruin a lot of blooms if you're determined to be successful.

Crafting

Air-dried honeysuckle blossoms bring a sweet fragrance to potpourris. Pressed blooms dry with an interesting shape and bring a light fragrance to your correspondence when used to decorate stationery. Fresh-cut honeysuckle vines can be entwined into a circle and secured with floral wire and then allowed to dry in place to create lovely wreath bases.

Hyacinth
HYACINTHUS

A native of Asia, these Dutch-cultivated bulbs provide magnificent flower heads with a sweet fragrance in white, pink, red, purple, blue, and yellow.

Growing and Landscaping

Plant hyacinth bulbs in the fall about 6" (15 cm) deep and 6" apart in well-drained soil in full sun. (They will not tolerate wet soils.) Heights average 8 to 10" (20 to 25 cm). After five or six years they will decline and should be replaced. Do not remove the foliage after blooming because this is how the plant prepares blooms for the next year. For the best display, plant clusters of at least five of the same color and variety together. They are excellent for use in front of foundation plantings, along walks and paths, in borders, and around trees and posts. They also make nice container plantings near doors or under windows for maximum enjoyment of their delightful fragrance.

Harvesting and Drying

Harvest at the peak of bloom, double-checking to make sure they are thoroughly dry to prevent browning. Enjoy the fragrance of the fresh-cut flowers for a few days, then put them in a desiccant to dry.

Crafting

Use hyacinth blooms in large spring wreaths and arrangements. Combine the blooms with daffodils and crocus for a sunny, spring effect.

Hydrangea
HYDRANGEA

This deciduous, perennial shrub features large clusters of showy flowers in pink, white, and blue. The varieties vary in size from 2 to 12' (.6 to 3.6 m). The white, old-fashioned types *(Hydrangea Paniculata)* that darken to mauve tend to dry the best.

Growing and Landscaping

Hydrangeas thrive best in rich, moist soil in an open area. They should be pruned severely in the spring to encourage strong shoots for good flower heads. H. Paniculata is one of the hardiest varieties, growing to the size and shape of a small tree. This variety has long panicles of white flowers and is attractive as a specimen shrub in a shrub border.

Harvesting and Drying

Hydrangea blooms can be harvested in the fall over several weeks: first when they are a creamy white, then a few weeks later when they are tinged with pink, and then again in a week or two when they have become a lovely shade of mauve. Be extra careful to harvest the blooms when they have no dampness on the blooms to prevent the flower heads from browning.

To dry, stand the blooms in a vase and enjoy them as an arrangement as they dry. You may also opt to hang them upside down in small bunches or to separate them into individual florets and press them. The blooms can be dried in the microwave for three to four minutes on a medium setting; they will shrink to about half of their fresh-cut size and the color stays true.

Crafting

Large wreaths made entirely from hydrangea panicles are stunning. They also make good filler material in wreaths and arrangements, and add a Victorian touch to Christmas swags and wreaths. Large clusters of dried hydrangea can be tucked into Christmas tree branches with stunning results. Another craft option is to break the large flower heads into smaller groupings. All dried hydrangeas can be enlivened with a light coat of gold glitter spray.

Iris

IRIS

Named after the mythological Iris (goddess of the rainbow), this perennial has been hybridized to provide a large selection of cultivars to choose from. All bearded iris have sword-shaped, grey-green leaves in a fan pattern, and their large, showy flowers bloom for three weeks in April to June (depending on the variety) and come in all colors and combinations. Japanese iris bloom later in the season (June or July) and come in white, blue, pink, and purple. Its dark green, swordlike leaves remain attractive all season and often reach heights of 3 to 4' (.9 to 1.2 m) tall.

Growing and Landscaping

Bearded iris need a well-drained soil that's high in organic matter, full sun, and a good fertilizing in early spring and again after blooming has finished. Allow 12 to 18" (30 to 46 cm) for spacing. Japanese iris thrive in wet areas and will take full sun or partial shade.

Iris may be interspersed in the perennial border, providing bright color before many other perennials begin to bloom. Dwarf varieties work well as edging plants, and mass plantings produce spectacular effects.

Harvesting and Drying

Harvest when the blooms are fully open and at their peak, double-checking to make sure they are completely free from moisture. The lighter shades tend to dry better than darker ones. Drying in the microwave for four to five minutes on a medium setting produces good color and shape results.

Air-drying works with some varieties with about 50% shrinkage, but it's worth experimenting. When more perfect blooms are desired, desiccant drying may be a better choice.

Crafting

Iris blooms work well in combination with other dried flowers for almost any spring craft, but unless they've been desiccant dried, they're not good choices for focal flowers.

Larkspur
DELPHINIUM

The annual species of delphinium, larkspur features tall (2 to 4', .6 to 1.2 m), showy spikes of blossoms in shades of blue, lilac, pink, and white. Larkspur enjoys the same stately beauty and elegance as perennial delphinium but it is easier to grow and has a much longer bloom time.

Growing and Landscaping

Plant larkspur in full sun with 12" (30 cm) spacing and in rich, well-drained soil that has been enriched with organic matter. Some of the tall varieties may require staking, but they are well worth the effort. Remove spent blooms to encourage abundant blooming. Mulch the roots to keep them cool in summer heat.

A bed of larkspur creates a nostalgic statement of elegance. The taller varieties are nice in the background of perennial borders or annual beds. Rather than planting them singly, always group them in at least threes to make a stronger statement. Midsize larkspurs in the middle of the perennial bed provide blues and pinks in areas where perennials have finished their bloom season.

Harvesting and Drying

Air-dry the spikes upside down in small bunches, taking care to position them with excess space to prevent crushing. For more curved stems, air-dry them upright. Expect the blooms to shrink about 25%; the light blues, pinks, and whites will retain their fresh-cut colors very well, while the dark blues deepen a shade or two.

Microwaving for four to five minutes on a medium setting produces slightly smaller blooms with good color retention. Individual blossoms, entire spikes, and the foliage may be pressed.

Crafting

Larkspur is an excellent choice for arrangements needing long sprays of color. In wreaths, arrange stems of larkspur in clusters of three for stunning results. The blooms combine well with other flowers with rich colors — roses, zinnias, and coneflowers.

Lavender
LAVANDULA

Known for its fresh fragrance, this perennial features cool gray-green foliage and slender, arching flower stems. Many varieties are available, with considerable size and color differences.

Growing and Landscaping

Lavenders are heat resistant and like full sun and a well-drained soil. They should be cut back in early spring just below last year's growth. If the blossoms are picked, many varieties will bloom all season. Hardy to zone 5, depending on the variety. Lavender is stunning when planted in large clumps of the same variety for a very formal effect, or with mixed varieties for a more natural look. They work well along walkways, borders, or as small hedges. Averaging 18" (46 cm), the smaller varieties are ideal for use in window boxes and planters, while the taller varieties (up to 3', .9 m) make good specimens in herb gardens and English cottage gardens.

Harvesting and Drying

Harvest at the peak of bloom when they are fully open, then air-dry upside down in small bunches or upright for more curving stems. Do not overdry. Some varieties may be pressed if they are not too succulent. Microwave drying is not advised because of the scent loss.

Crafting

Lavender stalks can be broken down into smaller segments for use in sachets, potpourris, perfumes, and bath oils, or to decorate guest soaps. The larger stalks make fragrant additions to wreaths, arrangements, and tussie mussies.

Liatris (Blazing Star)
LIATRIS SPICATA

A native American wildflower, perennial liatris features tall purple, lavender, and rose spikes. The tiny, individual blooms are densely packed along the upper 15 to 30" (38 to 75 cm) of the stems, making this plant a wonderful vertical accent in the garden. Liatris attracts butterflies and goldfinches during its July to September bloom season.

Growing and Landscaping
Liatris likes full sun or partial shade and docs well in most soils. The plant often self-seeds but is not invasive and should be divided in early spring every three or four years for rejuvenation. Liatris is excellent for wild garden settings, near ponds, or planted in groups of three in a mixed perennial border.

Harvesting and Drying
Harvest when the spikes are fully open at the pcak of bloom. Liatris air-dries easily by hanging upside down in small bunches with good color, size, and form retention. To microwave, place a bloom in a bag and place the bag over a bowl; cook on a medium setting for eight minutes. Liatris is not suitable for pressing.

Crafting
Liatris' strong, vertical blooms make beautiful focal flowers in arrangements. The stems are strong and will self-pick into floral foam and wreath bases. Large harvest wreaths are a good way to showcase liatris.

Lily of the Valley
CONVALLARIA MAJALIS

Native to Europe and Asia, this low-growing (8 to 10", 20 to 30 cm) perennial is a member of the lily family and naturalizes well in gardens. The graceful spikes of fragrant, creamy white, bell-shaped blossoms are frequently used for corsages, bridal bouquets, and small vase arrangements.

Growing and Landscaping
Plant in partial to full shade spaced 6 to 12" (15 to 30 cm) apart in an area where you won't mind their rapid spreading. Lily of the valley makes a wonderful addition to shade gardens, woodland gardens, rock gardens, and under trees where grass often refuses to grow. Try to plant some in an area you frequent in the spring so you can enjoy the wonderful sweet aroma. Hardy to -30 F.

Harvesting and Drying
Harvest when the blooms have fully opened. Upright air-drying in a vase preserves the fragrance. The blooms can be microwaved on a paper towel for three minutes on a medium setting; they shrink to about half their fresh-cut size and keep their lovely bell shape. Pressing and desiccant drying work well; air-drying does not.

Crafting
Air- and silica-dried blooms are excellent for tussie mussies, wreaths, arrangements, and any bridal decoration. The pressed blooms look especially lovely when combined with pressed ferns.

Love-in-a-Mist
NIGELLA

Nigella's common name, love-in-a-mist, comes from the feathery, threadlike bracts that surround the pink, blue, or white blossoms.

Growing and Landscaping
Love-in-a-mist needs full sun, good drainage, and monthly fertilizings. It does not transplant well, but the seeds can be sown 8 to 15" (20 to 39 cm) apart throughout the summer to ensure continuous blooms. Love-in-a-mist usually grows to 1-1/2 to 2' (.45 to .6 m) in a rather sprawly fashion and does not adapt well to formal situations. In cottage gardens or mixed borders, though, the plants are lovely. Include love-in-a-mist in the cutting garden.

Harvesting and Drying
Harvest stems of love-in-a-mist when the seed pods have ripened and air-dry by hanging. (Although the blossoms can be air- or desiccant-dried, they are not the plant's main attraction.) Do not microwave.

Crafting
Love-in-a-mist's creamy-colored seed pods feature intriguing purple striping. The pods make a truly beautiful and unusual accent in harvest wreaths, arrangements, swags, and garlands.

Marigold
TAGETES

A native of Mexico, this well-known annual features colorful blooms ranging from yellow to orange, bronze, and many combinations.

Growing and Landscaping

Plant marigolds in full sun in a well-drained soil with 6 to 18" (15 to 46 cm) spacing, depending on the variety. They do not need pampering and will tolerate dry conditions. Beware of over-fertilizing — it increases the foliage and decreases the blooms. Some varieties reseed themselves.

The dwarf varieties (6", 15 cm) are great for mass plantings, as edgings and border plantings along walks, and mixed with annuals in container plantings. The taller varieties are effective interspersed in the perennial border to add brilliant, season-long color in areas where other perennials have completed their blooming cycle. (Taller varieties (2 to 3', .6 to .9 m) may need to be staked to prevent wind and rain damage.)

Harvesting and Drying

Marigold blooms can be harvested any time before the blooms begin to fade. All varieties air-dry well by hanging upside down or on a screen. The flowers will shrink 30 to 40% and the colors will darken slightly. For use in arrangements, wire the stems before drying.

Microwave drying increases the shrinkage amount, but the colors hold well; microwave on a medium setting for six to seven minutes. For perfect color and shape retention, use a desiccant. Marigolds do not press well.

Crafting

Bright, colorful marigold blooms add a cheerful note to all types of floral crafts, especially harvest wreaths and arrangements.

Oriental Poppy
PAPAVER ORIENTALIS

Known for their large, crepe-papery blooms and coarse, toothed leaves, more than 60 cultivars of this popular perennial are sold. The flowers, which have a comparatively short bloom time, range from 4 to 10" (10 to 25 cm) in diameter, and their colors range in pinks, reds, whites, and oranges.

Growing and Landscaping

Averaging 2 to 4' (.6 to 1.2 m), Oriental poppies are widely used in borders, beds, and rock gardens. The foliage dies down when the blooming cycle ends, so the plants should be interplanted with summer-blooming annuals or perennials. Baby's breath works especially well. Hardy to zone 2.

Poppies must be in well-drained soil to prevent crown rotting, and the plants need full to partial sun. Plant them 18" (46 cm) apart. Mature plants should be divided every five years to rejuvenate the plant. Propagate by root division in the early fall, then plant the root crowns 3" (7.5 cm) below soil level.

Harvesting and Drying

Remove the petals separately before they begin to brown and air-dry them on a screen. For the seed pods, harvest them with their long stems intact after all the petals have fallen. Tie a square of cheesecloth around the pods to catch the seeds, then hang them upside down to dry.

Crafting

The deep red petals add color to potpourris, while the seed pods add a woodsy flair to arrangements, wreaths, and swags. The sturdy stems do not need reinforcing with wire, and the pods can also be accentuated with craft spray paint.

Pansy
VIOLA TRICOLOR

Descendants of woodland violets, pansies are sometimes still known by their old-fashioned name of heartsease. They come in a wondrous variety of colors, including white, yellow, red, pink, purple, bronze, and many combinations. The flowers bloom from May through July.

Growing and Landscaping

Pansies prefer well-drained, rich soil, moist conditions (they do not tolerate heat well), and full to partial sun. Mulch the soil to keep the roots cool and keep them well watered. Remove the spent blossoms to prolong blooming.

Pansies range in height from 4 to 9" (10 to 22 cm) and are best purchased as bedding plants. Pansies may reseed themselves or survive mild winters since they are highly cold resistant.

Pansies work well as edgings, in containers, and in rock gardens. When selecting planting sites, remember that pansies will go into severe decline during hot summer days.

Harvesting and Drying

Pansy blooms retain their color and shape very well in desiccants. Dried facedown in the microwave for two to three minutes on a medium setting, they keep their color and shape well but shrink to almost half of their fresh-cut size. Pansies can also be dried on a screen; expect significant shrinkage, darkened color, and some curling. Perhaps the ideal way to dry pansies is by pressing them.

Crafting

Dried pansies make lovely additions to potpourris, wreaths, picture frames, hats, tussie mussies, and candle rings. Pressed pansies add colorful beauty to pressed flower pictures.

Pearly Everlasting
ANAPHALIS

This hardy perennial is often chosen by gardeners for its silver-white, wooly leaves. The plant blooms from July through September with clusters of silver-white, ball-like flowers.

Growing and Landscaping

Pearly everlasting likes a well-drained soil and full sun or partial shade. The plants, which can grow to 3' (.9 m), should be spaced 14" (36 cm) apart. The plants can be increased by division in the spring. Hardy to zone 5.

Pearly everlasting makes a beautiful addition to rock gardens, perennial borders, and cutting gardens.

Harvesting and Drying

Harvest the flowers just before they mature. Drying with any one of the air-drying methods will give good color, form, and size retention. Pearly everlasting is not suitable for pressing, and there's not much point to using the microwave or a desiccant since it air-dries so well.

Crafting

Many gardeners grow pearly everlasting specifically for winter craft projects. For smaller projects, the flower clusters can be easily broken into smaller segments.

Peony
PAEONIA

This easily grown perennial can grow to 3' (.9 m) tall and is one of the longest lived of all perennials. Its large flowers bloom in May and June and come in shades of red, pink, white, and yellow. The glossy foliage is also attractive.

Growing and Landscaping

Plant peonies 1" (2.5 cm) below the soil so the eyes face up. (They are very particular about planting depth.) Peonies do best in full sun (but will tolerate light shade), with 2 to 3' spacing (.6 to .9 m). They do not do well in subtropical regions of the south. Fertilize annually in the spring, and remove dead foliage from the garden in the fall to prevent disease problems.

Peonies are effectively used in the border with other perennials, especially when grouped as accents. They are also attractive planted in hedges or rows, along fences, and in the cottage border.

Harvesting and Drying

Harvest peonies from the bud stage to just fully open for a variety of bloom forms. They air-dry well by hanging upside down in small bunches. The colors will darken by several shades and the blooms shrink about 50%, but they are still attractive. To microwave, cut the stem short and insert it through a paper towel with a hole in it to keep the bloom facing upward. Cook for six minutes on a medium setting.

Many crafters dry the foliage to use as filler material in arrangements. (Wire the stems before drying if this is your plan.) For more perfect retention of color and form, dry them in silica gel or sand. Peonies do not press well.

Crafting

Peonies make a wonderful, large focal flower in arrangements. The medium pink varieties are particularly attractive. The closed buds look lovely in combination with blossoms in wreaths and arrangements.

Plumed Celosia
CELOSIA PLUMOSA

Native to Africa, this vertical, feathery annual flower with a flamelike appearance comes in shades of yellow, orange, red, pink, and purple. Many cultivars are available, offering sizes from 6 to 36" (15 to 91 cm), some with variegated foliage. The plant blooms from June through October and makes a long-lasting and unusual cut flower.

Growing and Landscaping

Ideally, plant celosia in a rich, well-drained soil in full sun with 6 to 12" (15 to 30 cm) spacing. The plant will tolerate a poor, dry soil.

Plumed celosia works well in a mixed border, in containers with other annuals (especially marigolds), alone in massed beds, or as edging plants (dwarf varieties only).

Harvesting and Drying

Harvest celosia blooms at their peak and hang them in small bunches to dry. Expect good color and shape retention. Upright air-drying also works, but the plumes tend to spread apart and curve. The blooms can also be dried in the microwave for five to six minutes on a medium setting.

Crafting

The rich colors of plumed celosia make them ideal for harvest wreaths. Their interesting, feathery shape makes a nice addition to arrangements and swags. The plumes can be broken into smaller segments for use in all floral crafts and potpourris. A vase filled only with dried celosia is striking.

Pot Marigold
CALENDULA OFFICINALIS

Native to the Mediterranean region, these single (daisylike) and double (chrysanthemumlike) blooms come in shades of pure white, ivory, gold, orange, yellow, and peach. The foliage is an attractive dark green, ranging in height from 10 to 24" (25 to 60 cm), depending upon the variety. Pot marigolds are not related to the marigold.

Growing and Landscaping

Pot marigolds are one of the easiest annuals to grow and they bloom over a very long period. They should be planted in average soil in sun or semishade, spacing about 15" (39 cm) apart. It self-sows in the garden and will naturalize in mild climates.

Pot marigolds are good for mass bed plantings, for border plantings, container plantings mixed with other annuals, and interspersed in the front of the perennial border. The flowers grow on long stems that are ideal for cut flowers.

Harvesting and Drying

Harvest pot marigolds when they are just fully opened and at their blooming peak, double-checking to make sure there is no dampness to prevent browning. They air-dry well hanging upside down or on a screen, with some color darkening, about 25% shrinkage, and some petal curling. To microwave, cook for two minutes on a medium setting; check for dryness and add additional time if needed. For the most perfect retention of color and form, dry the blooms in a desiccant.

Crafting

Use these bright blooms in wreaths, garlands, arrangements, or anywhere else a strong colorful accent is desired. The blooms look nice when used with such richly colored blooms as zinnias and delphiniums.

Roses

ROSACEAE

Grown by the ancient Greeks, roses are certainly among the most widely grown and beloved of all flowers. Thousands of varieties have been developed, from 6" (15 cm) miniatures to towering climbers, blooming in every imaginable color except true blue.

Growing and Landscaping

All rose varieties should be should be well fertilized and watered, especially during dry spells. Plant them in fertile, well-drained soil; most varieties prefer full sun, although some will tolerate shade.

Often planted in formal beds, roses are also appealing in a mixed perennial border, trailing over trellises and arbors, or planted as a hedge.

Harvesting and Drying

Roses with smaller, well-formed buds and flowers dry the best, and pink roses retain their color most perfectly. Whites tend to turn cream-colored and reds will darken to maroon.

For air-drying, harvest the blooms from bud stage to half open, double-checking to make sure they are free from moisture. Air-dry by hanging or on a screen. They darken somewhat but retain much of their fresh-cut fragrance.

Microwaving open blooms for four to five minutes and buds for three to four minutes on a medium setting produces interesting results. The outer petals fold in, giving a sort of side view. Desiccant drying gives the best color and shape retention.

Crafting

Entire wreaths of rose blooms and buds are very striking; occasional blooms on twig wreaths, picture frames, topiaries, and tussie musses are also lovely. The fragrant petals, of course, are prized in potpourris.

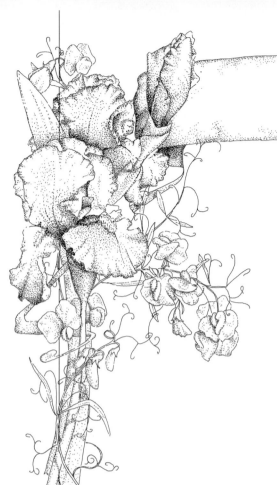

Salvia

SALVIA XSUPERBA

Known for its tall spikes of tiny flowers, this perennial member of the mint family blooms in shades of purple, blue, or pink throughout the gardening season. The aromatic leaves are on multi-branched plants which grow 2 to 3' (.6 to .9 m) tall.

Growing and Landscaping

Salvia looks nice in individual beds, in herb gardens, as edging plants, or in mixed perennial borders. Plant salvia in full sun, 1 to 2' (.3 to .6 m) apart. Although salvia can endure poor soil, drought, and heat, it does not do well in wet soil. Propagate by division or stem cuttings in the spring. Remove the spent blossoms to encourage prolific flowering. Hardy to zone 5.

Harvesting and Drying

Harvest your salvia when the blooms have just fully opened, or when the tops of the spikes are still in bud for a nice effect. Salvia dries well with hanging upside down in small buncles. The pink varieties dry particularly well.

Salvia blossoms can be pressed individually with good results. Dried in the microwave for five minutes at a medium setting, the flowers keep their shape and color well, except for the red varieties, which darken to almost black.

Crafting

Salvia is a great choice for herbal garlands, swags, hats, wreaths, baskets, and arrangements. The spiked blooms also work well on smaller projects such as decorative birdhouses, miniature baskets, and picture frames. This nostalgic, sweet-scented annual blooms in shades of white, pink, salmon, red, blue, lavender, and purple. The bushy, dwarf varieties average 18" (46 cm) tall, while the climbers can reach heights of 10' (3 m).

Growing and Landscaping

Sweet peas should be planted in fertile, well-drained soil in full sun. Water and fertilize well. Heat-tolerant varieties have been developed, but the soil still needs mulching to keep the roots cool. Remove all spent blossoms to promote abundant blooming.

Shasta Daisy
CHRYSANTHEMUM XSUPERBUM

The profusion of white flowers with yellow-eye centers has made this perennial plant a garden favorite. Single and double flower varieties are available, and they bloom from June until frost. The bushy plant grows 2 to 4' (.6 to 1.2 m) high with narrow, dark green leaves.

Growing and Landscaping
Plant shasta daisies in fertile soil in full sun or partial shade, spaced 12 to 24" (30 to 60 cm) apart. Remove the spent blossoms to prolong flowering and water well during drought conditions. Propagate by division in the spring to restore the plant's vigor. Hardy to zone 5.

Daisies are a wonderful addition in the perennial border or in an all-white perennial bed. Be sure to include a stand of daisies in the children's garden.

Harvesting and Drying
Harvest the blooms any time before they fade. Air-drying methods result in shriveled petals, while microwaving causes browning. Pressing and desiccant drying are the best choices; if you plan to use the daisies in an arrangement, wire the stems before drying for added versatility.

Crafting
Wreaths, hats, garlands, swags, and candle rings all benefit from the addition of shasta daisies, and the blooms look especially nice combined with globe amaranth and strawflowers. The individual petals look nice in potpourris.

Snapdragons
ANTIRRHINUM MAJUS

This popular annual features tapering spikes of blooms in pinks, reds, yellows, oranges, and bronzes, blooming from May through frost.

Growing and Landscaping

Snapdragons like full sun in rich, well-drained soils. They are heat tolerant and often reseed themselves. Space 6 to 12" (15 to 30 cm) apart. Remove spent blooms for more branching and abundant blossoms, and be sure to stake the taller varieties to prevent wind and rain damage.

The tall varieties (36 to 48", 91 to 120 cm) are great for use in the back of a perennial border to add color when others have finished blooming. The dwarf varieties (6", 15 cm) are good as border edgings or in solid beds for maximum effect. Plant medium-height varieties (18 to 24", 46 to 60 cm) in drifts at the center of the border.

Harvesting and Drying

Harvest when the blossoms at the bottom of the spike are fully open and the top blossoms are still partly in bud form for an interesting effect. Hang upside down in small bunches and expect about 40% shrinkage and some color darkening. Microwave drying for four to five minutes on a medium setting results in good color and size retention. Full spikes or individual blossoms can be pressed.

Crafting

The tapering spikes add an interesting accent to wreaths, especially those with twig bases that will not be completely covered. They work well in groups of three, and look nice in combination with strawflowers in harvest wreaths. Individual blossoms can be separated for use in small crafts such as decorative birdhouses, picture frames, and tree ornaments.

Strawflowers
HELICHRYSUM BRACTEATUM

Native to Australia, these bright everlastings are considered the finest of all everlastings for the home garden. Strawflowers were beloved by the Victorians, and today there are still many paperweights in existence with strawflowers in them.

Growing and Landscaping

Strawflowers are easily started from seed or purchased bedding plants. Look for seed mixes containing only certain colors, such as shades of pink and red. The 1 to 3' (.3 to .9 m) plants bloom from late spring through frost, and do best in moist, well-drained soil and full sun. They are easy to care for: just water them moderately during dry spells.

Dwarf varieties are good for borders, but the taller standards require some staking to prevent flopping over and are best planted in a cutting garden with 12" (30 cm) spacing.

Harvesting and Drying

Harvest the blooms any time after the center petals open, cutting at the main stem. Tie the stems in small bundles and hang them upside down. If you plan to use the flowers in arrangements, insert a length of floral wire up through the hollow stem before drying. The blooms can also be dried for two to three minutes on medium power in the microwave.

Crafting

Strawflowers have virtually unlimited craft uses. They make great accents in clusters of three in wreaths and swags, and the tiny buds are good for small-scale decorating such as small baskets, holiday ornaments, and decorative birdhouses. The wired blossoms can be shaped in arrangements and baskets. Grow extra of the red and mauve shades for Christmas wreaths, decorations, and swags.

Sunflowers
HELIANTHUS ANNUUS

Sunflowers have long been adored by the young and young at heart. Native to North America, they are both heat and drought tolerant, and bloom from mid- to late-summer. Colors range from the ever-popular yellow to red, bronze, mahogany, and attractive blends.

Growing and Landscaping

Tall sunflowers (12 to 15', 4 to 5 m) (with 12 to 18") 30 to 46 cm, blooms) make spectacular, giant hedges. Plant them on the outside edge of the garden to prevent them from shading smaller plants. The mid-size varieties (6 to 8', 1.8 to 2.4 m tall with 5", 12 cm blooms) are nice specimens for the back of the perennial border, while the new dwarf varieties (4', 1.2 m tall with 4", 10 cm blooms) can be interspersed in the border for bursts of color.

Harvesting and Drying

Harvest dwarf sunflower blooms when they are fully open and dry by hanging them upside down or on a screen. The petals will curl slightly and shrink about 40% but retain their color quite well.

Harvest the giant sunflowers when the seeds are mature; dry them as you would dry a dwarf bloom, taking extra care to make sure they are in a dry area with good air circulation to prevent molding. Speed the air-drying process by microwaving on a medium setting for 11 minutes. Place a bowl under the bag to catch the moisture and change the bag about halfway through to prevent the bloom from reabsorbing the moisture.

Crafting

Dwarf sunflowers are great to use in fall wreaths and arrangements, herbal swags, projects for children's rooms, and in Halloween displays. The giant sunflower heads can be used alone as an outdoor wreath for the birds, or decorated with grains or other edible dried flowers. They also look nice indoors, especially in the kitchen, with corn husk "petals" added.

Sweet Alyssum
LOBULARIA MARITIMA

A native of the Mediterranean region, this low-growing annual averages 4 to 10" (10 to 25 cm) tall. The flowers bloom freely from early spring until late summer in shades of blue, pink, and white.

Growth and Landscaping
Plant sweet alyssum in partial shade to full sun, 4 to 6" (10 to 15 cm) apart. Alyssum is an excellent choice for rock gardens and is often used as an edging plant and works well at the top of a wall where the sweet-smelling flowers can be appreciated. Alyssum also makes a nice plant for hanging baskets or an informal ground cover under taller plants such as roses.

Harvesting and Drying
Alyssum can be harvested any time before the flowers fade, and can be dried by hanging upside down in small bunches. Expect the colors to darken and the size to shrink about 50%. For pressing, break the flower heads into smaller blossoms. The blooms can be dried in the microwave for four minutes on medium power with good color and shape retention and little shrinkage.

Crafting
Alyssum makes a lovely and fragrant filler material in wreaths and garlands. The pressed blooms look especially nice on stationery and bookmarks.

Sweet Peas

LATHYRUS ODORATUS

This nostalgic, sweet-scented annual blooms in shades of white, pink, salmon, red, blue, lavender, and purple. The bushy, dwarf varieties average 18" (46 cm) tall, while the climbers can reach heights of 10' (3 m).

Growing and Landscaping

Sweet peas should be planted in fertile, well-drained soil in full sun. Water and fertilize well. Heat-tolerant varieties have been developed, but the soil still needs mulching to keep the roots cool. Remove all spent blossoms to promote abundant blooming.

Dwarf varieties are excellent for use in window boxes, and hanging baskets, and in massed beds. The taller varieties climb with short, wiry tendrils, and they showcase well on trellises, fences, posts, and screens.

Harvesting and Drying

Harvest sweet pea blooms any time before they begin to fade. For best color and shape retention, use a desiccant. Stems of sweet peas can also be hung upside down to air-dry; expect about 40% shrinkage and a darkening of color. Other drying options include pressing or microwaving for about three minutes on a medium setting.

Crafting

Stems of brightly colored, dried sweet peas look nice in spring wreaths, while the darker-colored stems look nice in harvest wreaths. The petals make pleasant additions to potpourris, while the pressed blooms work well with any type of pressed flower project.

Tulips
TULIPA

Originally introduced to Europe from Turkey, tulips are now commercially produced primarily in Holland. The satiny texture and interesting bell shape make them welcome symbols of spring's arrival.

Growing and Landscaping

A good way to plant tulips in large areas is to dig out the whole area to a depth of 6" (15 cm), place the bulbs in their desired positions with 4 to 6" (10 to 15 cm) spacing, add organic fertilizer, and then replace the soil. Remove the faded blossoms and allow the foliage to whither naturally.

Tulip plantings are most effective when one variety is planted in mass rather than mixing colors in one grouping. Plant them on hillsides, in woodland gardens, borders, or in beds that will later be planted with annuals.

Harvesting and Drying

Tulips are best dried in a desiccant for perfect retention of color and form. The very dark colors may darken even more as they dry. If you plan to use the dried tulips in an arrangement, wire the fresh-cut stems before drying. To microwave, gently stuff the center of the bloom with small balls of paper towels; cook on a paper towel for five minutes on a medium setting. Tulips do not air-dry or press well.

Crafting

Use tulips in spring wreaths, either alone or with daffodils, Dutch iris, and pussy willows.

Veronica
VERONICA

This hardy, free-flowering perennial comes in shades of blue, pink, purple, and white with the blooms densely arranged on narrow spikes at branch ends. Sometimes known as common speedwell, veronica blooms from late June through mid-August, and ranges in height from 12 to 30" (30 to 75 cm).

Growing and Landscaping

Plant veronica in well-drained soil in full sun or partial shade with 12 to 18" (30 to 46 cm) spacing, and remove the spent blossoms frequently to promote abundant blooming. Propagate every four years by division in spring or fall to rejuvenate the plant. Hardy to zone 4.

Veronica makes a decorative addition to the front of the perennial border, in sunny rock gardens, as a striking accent in the herb garden, or as an edging plant. Veronica's vertical spikes are best enjoyed when planted in clumps of at least three plants.

Harvesting and Drying

Harvest veronica when the top florets of the spikes are still in bud. They can be air-dried by hanging (for fairly straight stems) or upright (for curving, arching stems). Expect moderate shrinkage and good color retention.

Veronica blooms can be dried in the microwave for two to three minutes on a medium setting with results comparable to air-drying. Pressing works well.

Crafting

Veronica blooms add color and interesting shape to virtually any floral craft project, especially decorative birdhouses, picture frames, and small baskets.

Winged Everlasting
AMMOBIUM ALATUM

Native to Australia, this 2 to 3' (.6 to .9 m) annual herb bears a profusion of small white flowers with bright yellow centers from early summer through frost. The common name, winged everlasting, is derived from the interesting winged formation of the stems.

Growing and Landscaping

Winged everlastings are easy to grow and often reseed themselves in the spring. They prefer full sun and a sandy, well-drained soil. Winged everlastings make a nice addition to English cottage garden borders and in perennial gardens to add color and brightness throughout the summer and fall. Regular cutting of mature flowers encourages continued, profuse blooming.

Harvesting and Drying

The flowers may be harvested in bud or in full bloom before the centers have lost their bright yellow color. Strip off the leaves and hang the stems upside down in small bunches. If curving stems are desired, air-dry the stems upright.

Crafting

Since the flowers are quite small, they are wonderful to use in miniature decorations such as ornamental birdhouses, miniature baskets, and picture frames with dried miniature roses. Clustered in bunches, they make handsome accents in wreaths, straw hats, garlands, and herbal swags.

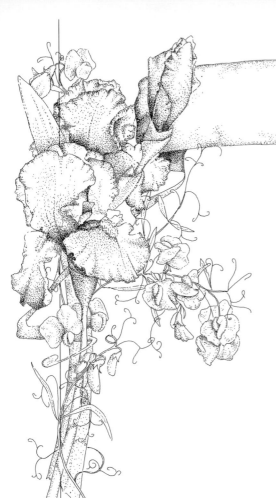

Yarrow
ACHILLEA

An easy-going perennial with soft, fernlike textured foliage, yarrow is attractive throughout the season. Various varieties bloom with flat, upward-facing flower heads of tiny blossoms in shades of white, golden-yellow, ruby red, salmon, rose pink, and bright yellow. The flowers are held on 18 to 24" (43 to 60 cm) stems, and the plants reach 2 to 4' (.6 to 1.2 m) tall.

Growing and Landscaping
Plant in full sun or light shade in well-drained, preferably dry soil of average fertility. (If the soil is too rich, growth tends to go to the foliage and there will be fewer flowers.) Propagate by division every four years in early spring to rejuvenate the plant; remove spent blossoms to promote flowering. Hardy in all zones.

Cluster three or more plants of the same variety together for a bushier appearance. Yarrow makes a nice accent in herb and rock gardens and in the perennial border.

Harvesting and Drying
Harvest the pinks and reds slightly before the blooms are fully open; harvest the yellows when the blooms are fully opened and at their peak. All yarrows dry well hung upside down in small bundles or in the microwave for two to three minutes on a medium setting. The golden-yellow and red varieties deepen in color as they dry, while the rose shades soften to a mauve/lavender. Shape and size retention is good.

Crafting
Because of their long, stiff stems, yarrow makes an excellent choice for multi-flower arrangements or just standing alone in a vase. The gold yarrows add a bold touch to fall wreaths. For smaller projects, break the flower heads down into segments.

Zinnia

ZINNIA ELEGANS

Prized by the Victorians, zinnias have been enjoyed as cut flowers for centuries. Zinnias come in both single and double blooms and in virtually every color except blue. They range in height from 6' (15 cm) dwarf varieties to 40" (100 cm). All varieties bloom from early summer until hard frost.

Growing and Landscaping

Zinnias seeds should be sown in fertile, well-drained soil in full sun. Thin or transplant them to 6 to 12" (15 to 30 cm) apart and fertilize regularly with a 5-10-10 fertilizer. Pinching the young plants will make them bushier with more prolific blooms.

Zinnias make excellent bedding and container plants. The tall varieties work well in the rear of a mixed border, while in the perennial garden they add season-long color. Zinnias also work well in cutting gardens or in herb gardens for color all season.

Harvesting and Crafting

Harvest zinnia blooms when they are fully open and dry them upside down in small bunches or on a screen. Expect the petals to curl, the colors to darken a shade or two, and about 50% shrinkage.

Drying zinnias in the microwave for three minutes on a medium setting tends to turn them brown. Silica gel drying gives the best color and shape retention. Single zinnia blooms are suitable for pressing.

Crafting

Zinnias add bright, cheerful accents to wreaths, arrangements, hats, and swags. They are particularly nice in harvest wreaths featuring an assortment of summer garden flowers. Single petals make colorful additions to potpourris.

Common/Botanical Name Index

American Bittersweet
Celastrus scandens

Annual Statice
Limonium sinuatum

Aster
Aster

Astilbe
Astilbe

Baby's Breath
Gypsophila paniculata

Bachelor Buttons
Centaurea Cyanus

Bee Balm
Monarda didyma

Black-Eyed Susan
Rudbeckia fulgida

Candytuft
Iberis umbellata

Carnation
Dianthus caryophyllus and Dianthus hybrids (cottage pinks)

Chrysanthemum
Chrysanthemum hybrids

Clematis
Clematis

Common Immortelle
Xeranthemum

Coneflower
Echinacea

Coreopsis
Coreopsis lanceolata

Crested Cockscomb
Celosia cristata

Crocus
Crocus

Daffodil
Narcissus

Dahlia
Dahlia

Delphinium
Delphinium

Dogwood
Cornus florida

Feverfew
Chrysanthemum parthenium

Foxglove
Digitalis

Geraniums
Pelargonium xhortorum

German Statice
Limonium dumosum

Globe Amaranth
Gomphrena globosa

Heather
Calluna vulgaris

Hollyhock
Alcea Rosea

Honeysuckle
Lonicera henryi or Lonicera japonica "Halliana"

Hyacinth
Hyacinthus

Hydrangea
Hydrangea

Iris
Iris

Larkspur
Delphinium consolida and Delphinium ajacis

Lavender
Lavandula

Liatris (Blazing Star)
Liatris spicata

Lily of the Valley
Convallaria majalis

Love-in-a-Mist
Nigella

Marigold
Tagetes

Oriental Poppy
Papaver orientalis

Pansy
Viola tricolor

Pearly Everlasting
Anaphalis

Peony
Paeonia

Plumed Celosia
Celosia Plumosa

Pot Marigold
Calendula officinalis

Roses
Rosaceae

Salvia
Salvia xsuperba

Shasta Daisy
Chrysanthemum xsuperbum

Snapdragons
Antirrhinum majus

Strawflowers
Helichrysum bracteatum

Sunflowers
Helianthus annuus

Sweet Alyssum
Lobularia maritima

Sweet Peas
Lathyrus odoratus

Tulips
Tulipa

Veronica
Veronica

Winged Everlasting
Ammobium alatum

Yarrow
Achillea

Zinnia
Zinnia elegans

Index